Dec 2021

Kansas City, MO Public Library
0000188529655

INSIDE MLS

INTER MIAMI CF

BY ANTHONY K. HEWSON

SportsZone
An Imprint of Abdo Publishing
abdobooks.com

abdobooks.com

Published by Abdo Publishing, a division of ABDO, PO Box 398166, Minneapolis, Minnesota 55439. Copyright © 2022 by Abdo Consulting Group, Inc. International copyrights reserved in all countries. No part of this book may be reproduced in any form without written permission from the publisher. SportsZone™ is a trademark and logo of Abdo Publishing.

Printed in the United States of America, North Mankato, Minnesota
052021
092021

THIS BOOK CONTAINS RECYCLED MATERIALS

Cover Photo: Chris O'Meara/AP Images
Interior Photos: Jon Endow/Image of Sport/Newscom, 4–5; Marcio Jose Sanchez/AP Images, 6, 9, 10; Patrick Smith/Getty Images Sport/Getty Images, 13; PKS/AP Images, 15; Bill Hudson/AP Images, 16; Tony Gutierrez/AP Images, 19; PA Wire URN:51126511/Press Association/AP Images, 21; Wilfredo Lee/AP Images, 23, 35, 37; Daniel A. Varela/TNS/Newscom, 25; Rich von Biberstein/Icon Sportswire/Newscom, 27; Douglas Cuellar/Zuma Press/Newscom, 28–29; John Raoux/AP Images, 31; Rich von Biberstein/Icon Sportswire/Newscom, 33; Matt Slater/PA Wire URN:41769525Press Association/AP Images, 38; Mark Brown/Getty Images Sport/Getty Images, 40–41; Jim Rassol/AP Images, 42

Editor: Patrick Donnelly
Series Designer: Dan Peluso

Library of Congress Control Number: 2020948268

Publisher's Cataloging-in-Publication Data
Names: Hewson, Anthony K., author.
Title: Inter Miami CF / by Anthony K. Hewson
Description: Minneapolis, Minnesota : Abdo Publishing, 2022 | Series: Inside MLS | Includes online resources and index.
Identifiers: ISBN 9781532194733 (lib. bdg.) | ISBN 9781098214395 (ebook)
Subjects: LCSH: Soccer teams--Juvenile literature. | Professional sports franchises--Juvenile literature. | Sports Teams--Juvenile literature.
Classification: DDC 796.334--dc23

TABLE OF CONTENTS

CHAPTER 1
WORTH THE WAIT 4

CHAPTER 2
BUILD IT WITH BECKHAM 14

CHAPTER 3
HEROIC HERONS 24

CHAPTER 4
MAKING MIAMI MEMORIES 34

TIMELINE	44
TEAM FACTS	45
GLOSSARY	46
MORE INFORMATION	47
ONLINE RESOURCES	47
INDEX	48
ABOUT THE AUTHOR	48

CHAPTER 1

WORTH THE WAIT

In a sea of black, a splash of pink stood out. For the players of Club Internacional de Fútbol Miami—more commonly known as Inter Miami CF—playing their first game as a team, it was a welcome sight. A small but dedicated group of supporters traveled all the way to Los Angeles to cheer them on.

The Miami players needed the support. Los Angeles Football Club (LAFC) was known for having some of the most passionate fans in Major League Soccer (MLS). They dressed mostly in black and sang and chanted throughout the game. It was a tough way for a new club to enter the league. But it would be a good test of how prepared Inter Miami was for its first official match.

Inter Miami forward Robbie Robinson, left, is challenged by LAFC defender Eddie Segura in Miami's first MLS match.

David Beckham looks on from his suite as Inter Miami makes its MLS debut in Los Angeles.

The referee blew his whistle. On March 1, 2020, Miami took the kickoff to officially begin its history. The players began the match hoping to become just the fifth MLS team ever to win its first game.

PINK ARMY

It made sense that Miami fans were excited to watch their new team. They had already waited 19 years. Miami's first MLS team folded in 2001. That left the area without top-level soccer.

It took an unlikely person to bring soccer back to South Florida. David Beckham was a legendary soccer player from England. He had no ties to Miami, but he chose it as the location for a new team he purchased in 2013. That began a long process of finding a site for a new stadium and determining how to pay for its construction. Finally in 2018, it became official. Miami was coming back to MLS.

Excitement had been building ever since. When the 2020 schedule came out and showed a road game to begin the season, some fans booked flights to Los Angeles. The day before the match, the team held a final practice. When the players returned to their hotel, the fans were there to welcome them with songs and chants.

Nearly 100 fans were ready to cheer on their new club early on match day. They waved flags as they marched to the stadium. With more than an hour remaining before kickoff, the supporters took their positions. Beckham was also in attendance and took pictures with the crowd.

STAR POWER

David Beckham is a big star on and off the field, well known even to people who aren't big soccer fans. Beckham's wife, Victoria, rose to fame in the 1990s as a pop singer. With Inter Miami's first game near Hollywood, some celebrity fans came out to support Beckham. Chef Gordon Ramsay and actresses Liv Tyler and Eva Longoria were in attendance to help cheer on Miami.

LAFC prided itself on its home-field advantage. The black-clad fans formed an intimidating match-day atmosphere. Miami midfielder Lee Nguyen knew that as well as anyone. He used to play for LAFC. He was impressed the visiting fans were able to make themselves heard.

"They were amazing, to travel all the way from the East Coast to LA and be able to show that kind of support," Nguyen said. "You could see all the pink in that corner over there and it was amazing. We felt that, and we hope they know we appreciate them for that."

SEEKING THREE POINTS

Miami's offense created some good chances. In the 42nd minute, star midfielder Rodolfo Pizarro was alone at the back post on a corner kick. His attempt was saved, but he got the ball back and played a cross to Nicolás Figal. However, Figal's header was stopped, too.

Lee Nguyen holds back former teammate and reigning MLS Most Valuable Player Carlos Vela in Inter Miami's opener.

In the other goal, Miami keeper Luis Robles stayed busy. LAFC peppered the net with 19 shots. Ten were on target. Only one got past the veteran keeper, but it was a big one.

Minutes after Miami's great chances on the offensive end, its defense had a letdown. It allowed skilled LAFC forward Carlos Vela too much space. Vela got the ball at the top of the penalty area. He looked up and saw Robles was a little too far out of the net.

Inter Miami goalkeeper Luis Robles, *right*, watches a shot by LAFC's Diego Rossi skip wide of the net.

Vela chipped a ball up in the air as Robles raced back to the goal line. He was too late. All Robles could do was get a fingertip on the ball as it went in the goal. Miami went into the locker room down 1–0.

Both sides worked hard in the second half. Miami put up 15 shots of its own. Nguyen came on in the 68th minute for more offense. But time was running out.

Miami had one last chance in the 97th minute. Off a throw-in, Nguyen got the ball alone in the box. He lined up to put the ball on goal, but his shot was weak. It was an easy save for the LAFC keeper. The final whistle blew seconds later.

Miami played well. It hurt to lose that first game, but the players saw some bright spots as well. They also saw that they had a fan base that appreciated their efforts.

"It's great to have that sort of support," Robles said. "We want to play for them and make them proud. Felt like we did a decent job of doing that today, and it's only going to get better."

A GOAL

One more road game awaited Miami. It was back across the country in the nation's capital against DC United. Miami was still looking for its first goal. It didn't have to wait long.

Miami had its first shot on goal in the first minute. Then in the second minute, Robbie Robinson won the ball in midfield. He went on a weaving run toward the United goal. Then he passed to Lewis Morgan, who carried it to the right of the goal near the end line. Morgan crossed it to Pizarro, who blasted the ball into the top of the net for Miami's historic first goal.

After taking a lead into halftime, Miami pushed for a second goal. Morgan thought he had scored one, but defender Román Torres had committed a handball earlier in the play. The goal was disallowed, and Torres was given a red card. Shortly after Torres was sent off, United was granted a penalty kick for a foul in the box. They converted it, and just like that the game was tied.

Miami tried to hold on and at least secure a point in the standings. But just two minutes later, United scored again. Playing down a man made it too hard for Miami to mount a comeback, and it suffered a second straight defeat.

The players looked forward to getting a boost from their home crowd. But a global pandemic made that impossible. A new illness called COVID-19 was spreading across the country and throughout the world, forcing the postponement of the MLS schedule. Inter Miami would take the field in Florida in 2020, but it would be under very different circumstances.

Teammates congratulate Rodolfo Pizarro after he scored the first goal in Inter Miami history against DC United.

CHAPTER 2

BUILD IT WITH BECKHAM

The state of North American soccer in the 1970s was shaky. Success was fleeting. A team might play for a championship one year, only to relocate or fold a couple years later. Such was the case for the Washington Darts and many other teams in the North American Soccer League (NASL).

The Darts played for the 1970 NASL title, losing to the Rochester Lancers. But the team had financial problems and was gone by 1972. It moved to Miami, where the club was renamed first the Gatos, and then the Toros.

Playing at Miami's Orange Bowl stadium, the Toros gathered a small but dedicated fan base. They averaged a high of 7,340 fans per game in 1974, when they made a run to the NASL title game. In 1975 they were joined in Florida by

Miami Toros defender Ralph Wright (5) pushes New York Cosmos star Pelé out of his way in a 1976 match in Miami.

The Toros' Don Reis, *right*, is sent flying by Mike Connell of the Tampa Bay Rowdies on June 6, 1975, at the Orange Bowl in Miami.

the Tampa Bay Rowdies. Immediately the teams and their fans developed a fierce rivalry. The first meeting at the Orange Bowl on June 6, 1975, was a physical battle that resulted in a 1–0 Tampa victory.

"There's going to be blood when we play again," said Toros captain Ron Sharp before a rematch on June 11. "The Rowdies are experts at hitting people when the referee is not looking."

THE FLORIDA DERBY

The soccer rivalry between Tampa Bay and Miami began in the NASL in 1975. It continued after Miami's club moved to Fort Lauderdale and even survived as teams folded and joined different leagues. After the latest version of the Strikers folded in 2016, the future of the Florida Derby was uncertain. The Rowdies still existed, but they played in the minor leagues. The only way they could meet Inter Miami in a competitive match would be in the US Open Cup.

The Toros won that rematch in Tampa, 2–0. But it was also their last win in the rivalry. By 1976 the club's financial and attendance problems were becoming too much to handle. After that season, the team moved north to Fort Lauderdale, Florida, and became the Strikers.

There they found a better stadium. Lockhart Stadium was smaller and built just for soccer, unlike the Orange Bowl, which was home to Miami's successful professional and college football teams. The Strikers regularly packed Lockhart Stadium, playing there until 1983, when the team moved to Minnesota. But soccer lived on in Fort Lauderdale, as three more minor league teams bearing the Strikers name would play in the city over the next 40 years.

THE MIAMI FUSION

While minor league soccer continued in Fort Lauderdale, the city of Miami was without a top-level team to call its own for more than 20 years. That finally changed in the late 1990s. MLS played its first season in 1996. One year later it announced it was expanding for the first time. Both Chicago and Miami would join the league in 1998.

Miami was chosen because of South Florida's long history of supporting soccer at other levels. And Miami had a large Latin American population, a group that traditionally includes many soccer fans.

Miami's new team was called the Fusion. The team planned to play in the Orange Bowl, but it settled on Lockhart Stadium instead. Lockhart was the first soccer-specific stadium in MLS. Most other teams played in huge football stadiums. Lockhart had fewer seats, making its stands easier to fill.

The stadium was beyond full on March 15, 1998, for the first game in Fusion history. Led by star midfielder Carlos Valderrama and his wild mane of blonde hair, the Fusion faced off against two-time MLS champion DC United. A sellout crowd of 20,450 packed Lockhart Stadium while another 3,000 had to

Pablo Mastroeni (25) of the Miami Fusion battles with New England's Joe-Max Moore in a 1999 match.

be turned away. It was a carnival-like atmosphere to welcome top-level soccer back to South Florida.

Unfortunately, the Fusion couldn't manage a goal in a 2–0 loss. And Miami struggled to keep the stands filled on a consistent basis. Fans in Miami eventually tired of making the long trek to Fort Lauderdale to watch the games. Despite making a playoff appearance, the team averaged just over 10,000 fans per game. That number had slipped to less than 8,000 by 2000.

Rumors began to spread about the Fusion's uncertain future. Both the team and MLS were losing money. The league was talking about reducing from 12 teams to 10.

In the middle of this, the Fusion had their best season. They posted the best record in MLS in 2001 and attendance was up. But just before the 2002 season, the league confirmed it was folding two teams and Miami was one of them. The other was the Tampa Bay Mutiny, leaving Florida without top-tier soccer.

BECKS TO THE RESCUE

Having to eliminate two teams was the low point of MLS history. The league was struggling to survive. Cutting Miami and Tampa helped MLS reduce its expenses and slowly start to recover.

Then in 2007, global soccer star David Beckham signed with the Los Angeles Galaxy. He immediately brought star power and relevance to a league that was still finding its footing on

David Beckham, shown with his sons celebrating his second straight MLS Cup victory with the Galaxy in 2012, hoped to bring the same success to Inter Miami.

the US sporting scene. Beckham's influence helped the league greatly increase its popularity in the United States and around the world.

By the time Beckham played his last MLS game in 2012, the league was thriving. It had grown to 19 teams, 14 of which played in soccer-specific stadiums. The league also had a better national television contract, with more matches being televised coast to coast.

Beckham was as much a marketer for the league as he was a player. As part of his unique contract, he got the rights to purchase an expansion team for a reduced rate. And MLS was still looking to expand. Its plans included Miami.

MLS commissioner Don Garber publicly discussed his hope to return to Miami. Former Miami Fusion supporters' group the *Afusionados* began bombarding his office with emails, making sure he didn't forget about Miami.

Beckham retired as a player in April 2013. He then talked to MLS about buying an expansion team and where to place it. He got together with some investors from Miami, and the group started working on a bid.

Two major roadblocks stood in their way. The group needed land for a stadium. And they needed to be able to pay for it. For four years, Beckham's ownership group went back and forth with the city of Miami. MLS made it clear that it would not approve the bid without a real stadium plan.

But Beckham's confidence never wavered. "There never was one moment when I thought Miami was not the right place," he said.

Inter Miami majority owner Jorge Mas speaks to supporters as work begins at the site of the club's future stadium in 2019.

Finally on January 29, 2018, the owners had a proposal MLS could accept. Miami was officially awarded a new team to begin play in 2020. But the work of putting a team on the field—and deciding which field to play on—was just beginning.

CHAPTER 3

HEROIC
HERONS

David Beckham had played for some of the most glamorous soccer teams in the world. He began his career with Manchester United in his native England, and then he joined Real Madrid in Spain. Later in his career, he had stints with AC Milan in Italy and Paris Saint-Germain in France. So when it came time to build his own club, Beckham dreamed big. He wanted to sign world-class players.

But signing players like that wasn't easy in MLS. Unlike other soccer leagues, MLS limited how much its teams spent on players. They could sign Designated Players, whose salaries didn't count against the salary cap, but even that policy had its limits. Beckham had to set his sights a little lower, at least when assembling the club's first roster.

Matías Pellegrini passes the ball during Inter Miami's first practice at their new training site in February 2020.

Miami made a Designated Player one of its first-ever signings, bringing in Matías Pellegrini in July 2019. The 19-year-old midfielder from Argentina was not a big name, but he showed big promise. In just a few games in Argentina's top league, Pellegrini became a key player. He was a strong passer, and Miami had to outbid teams in Europe to get him.

Miami's second Designated Player was Rodolfo Pizarro. Many American soccer fans were more familiar with Pizarro. He was a rising star with the Mexico national team. Coach Diego Alonso also knew Pizarro well. He was Pizarro's coach with Monterrey of the Mexican league. Both men came to Inter Miami after the 2019 season.

A creative attacking midfielder, Pizarro could both score and set up goals. He scored the historic first goal in Miami history in the club's second match. He went on to score four total and added five assists in 19 games. At age 26, he was in

DIEGO ALONSO

Miami made an experienced choice when it hired Diego Alonso for its first head coach. Alonso had a long career as a player on three continents and with Uruguay's national team. Alonso went on to a successful managing career with some of the top teams in Mexico. Alonso was known for coaching an exciting attacking style that he hoped to bring to Miami.

Rodolfo Pizarro fights off two Atlanta United defenders in a September 2020 match.

the prime of his career and could help mentor younger players such as Pellegrini and 23-year-old Lewis Morgan.

Morgan had spent time in his native Scotland with Celtic. He even played in the prestigious European Champions League.

Inter Miami brought in US national team midfielder Wil Trapp, *right*, to provide leadership and experience.

Morgan was a good player for Celtic, but he also spent time out on loan to get more playing time. With Miami, he got the chance to be a full-time starter. The midfielder showed off his playmaking ability. His five goals and eight assists were the best on the team.

VETERAN LEADERSHIP

Inter Miami may have been low on big-name international stars. But it had several veteran players with international experience in key roles. Wil Trapp anchored midfield. The native of Columbus, Ohio, was the captain of his hometown

Crew, for which he played seven seasons. Trapp was one of the Crew's most beloved players and a leader in the locker room.

Trapp made more than 200 appearances for Columbus and was a 2016 All-Star. His ability to play deep in midfield and make plays would help kickstart Miami's scoring attack.

At forward, Inter traded for Juan Agudelo, another US national team veteran. Agudelo had played in MLS since 2010. He had spent most of his career in New England, where he scored 35 goals in six seasons. He also saw playing time overseas in the Dutch league. Agudelo ended up playing in 14 matches in 2020, scoring three goals.

To help lead its defense, Inter Miami locked up Román Torres. The captain of the Panama national team was an experienced pro in South America and in MLS. Torres was also known as a good teammate and leader.

In goal was veteran keeper Luis Robles. He was the oldest member of the inaugural team, but experience is important at that position. Robles was named the MLS Goalkeeper of the Year in 2015 when he played for the New York Red Bulls. He was as reliable as can be, at one point starting an MLS-record 183 games in a row. He ranked among the top 10 in

Román Torres looks to pass the ball in a July 2020 match.

league history in wins and shutouts. Robles was honored as the first captain in Miami team history.

ADDING STARS

The first Inter Miami squad may have been lacking big-name talent. But the club pulled together and chased a playoff spot throughout 2020. In August, the club acquired one of the international stars it had been seeking. Midfielder Blaise Matuidi joined Miami from Italian powerhouse Juventus.

One month later, Miami signed an even bigger name away from Juventus. Gonzalo Higuaín was one of the top goal scorers in the world. The striker had played for some of the biggest clubs in Europe. Higuaín was 32, but he was still a scoring threat. His 66 goals in three seasons for Juventus were second-most on the team.

Besides their playmaking ability, these two teammates knew how to win. Matuidi had won a World Cup with France in 2018. Higuaín had made the World Cup final with Argentina in 2014. Miami became the only club in MLS to have two World Cup finalists on its roster.

Higuaín and Matuidi helped boost Miami to a historic playoff spot in its first season. And they were expected to be

Luis Robles jumps high to make a save in a September 2020 match at Atlanta United.

key parts of the team's future. Meanwhile, Trapp, Agudelo, Torres, and Robles were all gone after the 2020 season as the club kept working toward building a world-class roster.

CHAPTER 4

MAKING MIAMI
MEMORIES

Seventeen years is a long time to wait for a soccer team. But once the birth of a Miami team was officially announced on January 29, 2018, suddenly there was very little time to get ready. The club was set to join MLS for the 2020 season.

All the team had was a future stadium site. It had no name, colors, coaches, players, or even a temporary place to play while the stadium was being built. It had barely two years to get all those things ready.

By the fall, fans at least knew what to call their club. On September 5, 2018, the team officially became Club Internacional de Fútbol Miami. The name, which translates to "Miami International Football Club," was a tribute to the

A mural in downtown Miami displays the club's badge and team colors.

Spanish-speaking population of Miami. Nearly three-quarters of Miami residents spoke Spanish at home.

The name also represented the team's goals. It didn't want to be just an American soccer team. It wanted to be a global one. The team planned to be world-class and bring in big-name players from around the world.

THE TWO HERONS

The same day, the club revealed the crest that all players would wear over their hearts. In the center were two birds with pink legs. Because flamingos are common in Florida, many people misidentified the birds. They were actually great white herons, another bird found in Florida.

Herons are known to be fierce hunters. They fight other birds for prey, even birds that are bigger and stronger. That made them a perfect symbol for a Miami soccer team.

The herons' legs intertwined to form a letter M for Miami. Above the birds was a setting sun. Florida is known as the Sunshine State. The sun had seven rays, a nod to the No. 7 that David Beckham wore as a player.

The pink color is popular in Miami architecture and design. The rest of the crest was black, which was the team's other

Diego Alonso, Inter Miami's first head coach, was introduced to the media in January 2020.

main color. The club and its design team went through almost 1,000 different sketches before settling on the right one. Each detail helped make a unique crest that represented Miami.

A GRAND ENTRANCE

The Fusion may have left in 2001, but soccer fans never disappeared from Miami. The supporters' group the *Afusionados* ceased to exist after 2001, but the members still

Lockhart Stadium had fallen into disrepair, so Inter Miami decided to demolish it and rebuild a temporary stadium on the site.

sometimes got together to watch other matches. Once it became official that MLS was coming back, the group reformed with a new name, the Southern Legion.

Two more supporters' groups formed in 2018—the Siege and Vice City 1896. Each group formed its own identity, but they were united in support of Inter Miami. As the team's debut drew closer, the fans wanted to let the rest of MLS know they were coming.

Orlando City was the only other MLS team in Florida. In 2018, it hosted the league's All-Star Game. Some Inter Miami supporters made the trip north for the match. They paraded into the stadium waving flags to represent their team.

WHAT'S OLD IS NEW

For a new home, Miami looked to a previous address. The Fusion's old home of Lockhart Stadium had sat empty since the last version of the Fort Lauderdale Strikers folded in 2016. With no team using it, the stadium started to fall apart and couldn't host soccer anymore. But the site was the perfect spot for a temporary stadium.

In April 2019, the club began clearing the site to build a temporary 19,000-seat stadium. It was designed to host the

Inter Miami CF Stadium hosted its first match in August 2020.

team for two seasons while Miami Freedom Park was built near the Miami airport. The temporary stadium would then become the home for Inter Miami's minor league team.

There would be a home for the supporters as well. The stadium was built with standing sections behind the goal for the most dedicated fans. They would help give Miami a home-field advantage even in a temporary home.

PLAYOFF PUSH

Miami never got the chance to play its home opener in front of fans. After two close road losses in March, MLS paused the season due to the COVID-19 pandemic. The league returned in July for the MLS Is Back Tournament in Orlando, but Miami lost all three games. It wasn't until August that the club finally got to play its home opener.

Julián Carranza and Matías Pellegrini celebrate one of Carranza's two goals in Inter Miami's first victory on August 22, 2020.

The game was an all-Florida matchup against Orlando City. For one night at least, the club's scoring woes seemed far behind. Julián Carranza and Rodolfo Pizarro formed a lethal scoring combo. Carranza scored twice and Pizarro added a third as Miami prevailed 3–2 for its historic first win.

Miami was able to keep playing well. The club did not score much, but it played strong defense. It only lost two games by more than one goal. Meanwhile, the scoring attack got a boost late in the year with the signing of Blaise Matuidi and Gonzalo Higuaín. And a few fans were even allowed to watch games inside the stadium late in the year.

Because of the disruption of the pandemic, MLS expanded the number of teams to make the playoffs. Miami was good enough to earn the final playoff spot. It faced fellow expansion team Nashville SC. However, Miami's scoring woes continued, and this time the defense had a rare bad game, too. Miami lost 3–0. But just making the playoffs was a big deal for an expansion team. Miami was only the seventh MLS team to make the playoffs in its first season.

The club had bigger goals in mind, though. It wanted to sign huge stars and compete for MLS Cups. Fans couldn't wait to see those plans take shape in the years ahead.

NEW BOSSES

Phil Neville replaced Diego Alonso as manager for the 2021 season. Neville was the manager of the England women's national team and had been a teammate of David Beckham's. The club also hired Chris Henderson as sporting director. Henderson had held the same job with the Seattle Sounders and led them to two MLS Cups.

TIMELINE

1976 — The NASL's Miami Toros, two years removed from an appearance in the Soccer Bowl, move up the coast to Fort Lauderdale.

1998 — The Miami Fusion makes its MLS debut. The club will fold after four seasons when the league contracts due to financial difficulties.

2013 — David Beckham retires as a pro soccer player in May and begins exploring his option to purchase an MLS expansion team, eventually deciding on Miami with a group of other investors.

2014 — On February 5, MLS announces Beckham has officially exercised his option to buy a new team and will lead an expansion bid for Miami.

2018 — After years of negotiations, MLS officially approves Miami as the 25th MLS team on January 29.

2018 — On November 6, Miami voters approve construction of Miami Freedom Park as the club's permanent home.

2019 — On July 26, Inter Miami signs its first two players, forward Julián Carranza and midfielder Matías Pellegrini, both 19-year-olds from Argentina.

2020 — Inter Miami plays its first MLS game on March 1, a 1–0 loss on the road against Los Angeles FC.

2020 — Rodolfo Pizarro scores the first goal in team history, but Miami loses its second match 2–1 at DC United on March 7.

2020 — Miami becomes the seventh MLS team to make the playoffs in its first season but loses 3–0 to Nashville.

TEAM FACTS

FIRST SEASON
2020

STADIUM
Inter Miami CF Stadium (2020–)

PLAYOFF APPEARANCES
2020

KEY PLAYERS
Juan Agudelo (2020)
Julián Carranza (2020–)
Gonzalo Higuaín (2020–)
Blaise Matuidi (2020–)
Lewis Morgan (2020–)
Matías Pellegrini (2020–)
Rodolfo Pizarro (2020–)
Luis Robles (2020)
Wil Trapp (2020)

KEY COACHES
Diego Alonso (2020)
Phil Neville (2021–)

GLOSSARY

commissioner
The chief executive of a sports league.

corner kick
A free kick from a corner of the field near the opponent's goal.

cross
A pass delivered from the side of the field toward the middle.

defender
A player whose job is to keep the other team from taking shots and scoring.

derby
An ongoing competition between two teams from the same region or city.

Designated Player
A player whose salary doesn't count against the salary cap, which allows teams to sign higher-priced stars.

expansion team
A new team that is added to an existing league.

folded
Went out of business.

penalty area
The box in front of the goal where a player is granted a penalty kick if he or she is fouled.

supporters' groups
Fan groups that stand and support their team throughout the game by singing, chanting, drumming, waving flags, and more.

MORE INFORMATION

BOOKS

Kortemeier, Todd. *Total Soccer*. Minneapolis, MN: Abdo Publishing, 2017.

Marthaler, Jon. *Ultimate Soccer Road Trip*. Minneapolis, MN: Abdo Publishing, 2019.

Marthaler, Jon. *US Men's Professional Soccer*. Minneapolis, MN: Abdo Publishing, 2019.

ONLINE RESOURCES

To learn more about Inter Miami CF, please visit **abdobooklinks.com** or scan this QR code. These links are routinely monitored and updated to provide the most current information available.

INDEX

Acosta, George, 30
Agudelo, Juan, 30, 33, 43
Alonso, Diego, 26, 43
Beckham, David, 7, 8, 20–22, 24, 43
Beckham, Victoria, 8
Carranza, Julián, 42
Figal, Nicolás, 8
Garber, Don, 23
Henderson, Chris, 43
Higuaín, Gonzalo, 32, 43
Longoria, Eva, 8

Matuidi, Blaise, 32, 43
Morgan, Lewis, 11–12, 27–28
Neville, Phil, 43
Nguyen, Lee, 8, 10–11
Pellegrini, Matías, 26–27
Pizarro, Rodolfo, 8, 11, 26–27, 42
Ramsay, Gordon, 8
Robinson, Robbie, 11
Robles, Luis, 9–11, 30, 32–33

Sharp, Ron, 16
Torres, Román, 12, 30, 33
Trapp, Wil, 29–30, 33
Tyler, Liv, 8
Valderrama, Carlos, 18
Vela, Carlos, 9–10

ABOUT THE AUTHOR

Anthony K. Hewson has followed American soccer since before the MLS days. Originally from San Diego, he now lives in the Bay Area with his wife and dogs.